Table of Contents

Chapter 1: The Evolution of AI and Quantum Technologies

The History of Artificial Intelligence

The history of artificial intelligence (AI) dates back to the 1950s when the term was first coined by computer scientist John McCarthy. AI is the simulation of human intelligence processes by machines, such as learning, problem solving, and decision making. Over the decades, AI has evolved significantly, with advancements in machine learning, deep learning, and neural networks driving its progress.

One of the key milestones in the history of AI was the development of expert systems in the 1970s and 1980s. These systems were designed to mimic the decision-making abilities of human experts in specific domains, such as medicine and finance. While expert systems showed promise, they were limited by their inability to adapt to new information or changing circumstances.

In the 1990s and 2000s, the focus in AI shifted towards machine learning and data-driven approaches. This led to the development of algorithms that could learn from large datasets and improve their performance over time. The rise of big data and cloud computing further accelerated the progress of AI, enabling researchers to train more complex models on vast amounts of data.

In recent years, AI has made significant strides in areas such as natural language processing, computer vision, and autonomous systems. Companies like Google, Microsoft, and Tesla have invested heavily in AI research and development, driving innovation in various industries. However, the rapid advancement of AI has also raised concerns about its impact on jobs, privacy, and security.

As countries around the world compete for technological superiority in AI and quantum technologies, the race for innovation is intensifying. The intersection of AI and quantum computing holds great potential for breakthroughs in areas such as cryptography, drug discovery, and climate modeling. To stay ahead in this global race, nations must invest in research, talent development, and strategic partnerships to harness the full potential of AI and quantum technologies for national security and economic prosperity.

The Rise of Quantum Computing

Quantum computing has emerged as a cutting-edge technology that has the potential to revolutionize the way we process information and solve complex problems. Unlike classical computers, which rely on bits to store and process data, quantum computers use quantum bits or qubits, which can exist in multiple states simultaneously. This allows quantum computers to perform calculations at speeds far beyond the capabilities of traditional computers.

The development of quantum computing has been driven by a combination of advances in physics, mathematics, and computer science. Researchers around the world have been working tirelessly to harness the power of quantum mechanics to build increasingly powerful quantum computers. Companies like IBM, Google, and Microsoft have made significant investments in quantum computing research, with the goal of developing practical quantum computing systems that can be used for a wide range of applications.

One of the key advantages of quantum computing is its ability to solve problems that are currently intractable for classical computers. For example, quantum computers have the potential to revolutionize fields such as cryptography, drug discovery, and climate modeling by enabling researchers to perform calculations that would take millions of years to complete on a traditional computer in a matter of seconds. This has led to a growing interest in quantum computing from governments, businesses, and research institutions around the world.

As the race for quantum supremacy heats up, countries are vying to establish themselves as leaders in this emerging field. The United States, China, and the European Union have all made significant investments in quantum computing research, with the goal of gaining a competitive edge in areas such as national security, economic competitiveness, and scientific discovery. The development of quantum computing is also raising important questions about the potential impact on international security and the need for global cooperation to ensure that this powerful technology is used responsibly.

In conclusion, the rise of quantum computing represents a major milestone in the ongoing global race for technological superiority. As countries around the world compete to develop the most powerful quantum computers, the implications for international security, economic competitiveness, and scientific discovery are profound. It is clear that quantum computing will play a key role in shaping the future of technology and innovation, and it is essential that policymakers, researchers, and industry leaders work together to harness the potential of this transformative technology for the benefit of all.

The Intersection of AI and Quantum Technologies

As we race towards the future, the intersection of artificial intelligence (AI) and quantum technologies is becoming increasingly significant. These two cutting-edge fields have the potential to revolutionize industries, reshape economies, and transform the way we live and work. The convergence of AI and quantum technologies is expected to unlock new possibilities and opportunities that were previously thought to be impossible.

AI, with its ability to analyze vast amounts of data and make predictions, has already shown tremendous potential in various applications such as healthcare, finance, and transportation. Quantum technologies, on the other hand, are poised to revolutionize computing, communication, and cryptography by harnessing the power of quantum mechanics. By combining the strengths of AI and quantum technologies, we can expect to see even more powerful and efficient systems that can solve complex problems at an unprecedented speed.

One of the key areas where the intersection of AI and quantum technologies is expected to have a significant impact is in the field of cybersecurity. As our reliance on digital technologies continues to grow, the need for secure and resilient systems has never been greater. By leveraging the capabilities of AI and quantum technologies, we can develop more advanced cybersecurity solutions that can adapt and evolve in real-time to counter emerging threats.

Furthermore, the intersection of AI and quantum technologies is also expected to revolutionize industries such as logistics, manufacturing, and energy. By using AI to optimize operations and quantum technologies to enhance computing power, companies can streamline processes, reduce costs, and improve overall efficiency. This convergence of technologies will not only drive innovation but also create new business opportunities and economic growth.

In conclusion, the intersection of AI and quantum technologies represents a new frontier in the global race for technological superiority. As countries and companies compete to develop and deploy these cutting-edge technologies, it is essential to consider the implications for international security. By understanding the potential risks and opportunities associated with the convergence of AI and quantum technologies, we can work towards harnessing the power of these technologies for the benefit of all. The future is here, and the time to embrace the possibilities of AI and quantum technologies is now.

Chapter 2: The Global Competition in AI and Quantum Technologies

The Leading Players in AI Development

When it comes to the development of artificial intelligence (AI), there are several countries that stand out as the leading players in this rapidly evolving field. These countries have made significant investments in AI research and development, and their efforts have paid off in the form of cutting-edge technologies and innovative applications that are shaping the future of AI.

One of the leading players in AI development is the United States. With its world-renowned tech companies like Google, Microsoft, and IBM leading the way, the U.S. has been at the forefront of AI research and development for decades. The country's strong academic institutions and robust funding for AI research have helped it maintain its position as a global leader in this field.

Another key player in AI development is China. The Chinese government has made AI a top priority, investing heavily in research and development and setting ambitious goals for the country to become a global leader in AI by 2030. Chinese tech companies like Baidu, Alibaba, and Tencent are also making significant contributions to the advancement of AI technology, pushing the boundaries of what is possible in this field.

In Europe, countries like the United Kingdom, Germany, and France are also emerging as leaders in AI development. These countries have strong research institutions and a growing ecosystem of AI startups that are driving innovation in this field. The European Union has also made AI a key focus of its digital strategy, aiming to position Europe as a global leader in AI and ensure that its citizens benefit from the opportunities that AI technology can offer.

Overall, the global race for technological superiority in AI is heating up, with countries around the world vying for leadership in this critical field. The leading players in AI development are investing heavily in research and development, forging partnerships with industry and academia, and setting ambitious goals for the future. As AI technology continues to advance at a rapid pace, these countries will play a crucial role in shaping the future of AI and driving innovation in this transformative field.

Quantum Supremacy: The Race to Build the Most Powerful Quantum Computer

In the global race for technological superiority, one of the most exciting and cutting-edge competitions taking place is the race to build the most powerful quantum computer. Quantum supremacy, as it is known, refers to the point at which a quantum computer can outperform even the most advanced classical supercomputers in certain tasks. This milestone has long been seen as a key indicator of progress in the field of quantum computing and a potential game-changer in fields such as cryptography, drug discovery, and materials science.

Several major players in the field of quantum computing are vying for supremacy, including tech giants like Google, IBM, and Microsoft, as well as research institutions and startups around the world. Google made headlines in 2019 when it claimed to have achieved quantum supremacy with its 53-qubit Sycamore processor, which performed a calculation in just 200 seconds that would have taken the world's most powerful supercomputer 10,000 years to complete. However, this claim has been met with skepticism and debate within the scientific community.

The race to build the most powerful quantum computer is not just about bragging rights or scientific achievement – it also has significant implications for national security and economic competitiveness. Quantum computers have the potential to revolutionize fields such as cryptography, making current encryption methods obsolete and posing a threat to the security of sensitive information. Countries around the world are investing heavily in quantum research and development in order to stay ahead in this new technological arms race.

In addition to the race for quantum supremacy, there is also a growing competition in the field of artificial intelligence (AI), which is closely linked to quantum technologies. Quantum AI algorithms have the potential to vastly outperform classical AI algorithms in certain tasks, leading to advances in machine learning, robotics, and other AI applications. As countries vie for dominance in both AI and quantum technologies, the stakes are higher than ever for global security and economic prosperity.

As the race to build the most powerful quantum computer heats up, it is clear that the winners will not only have bragging rights in the scientific community, but also a strategic advantage in the global competition for technological superiority. The implications of quantum supremacy extend far beyond the realm of quantum computing, with potential impacts on national security, economic competitiveness, and the future of AI. The global race for technological superiority is entering a new phase, and the winners will shape the course of history in the 21st century.

National Strategies for Advancing AI and Quantum Technologies

In the global race for technological superiority, nations around the world are increasingly recognizing the importance of advancing artificial intelligence (AI) and quantum technologies. These cutting-edge fields have the potential to revolutionize industries, improve national security, and enhance overall quality of life. As a result, many countries are developing national strategies to prioritize and accelerate the development of AI and quantum technologies.

One key component of national strategies for advancing AI and quantum technologies is investing in research and development. Governments are allocating significant funding towards research initiatives, partnerships with academia and industry, and the establishment of research centers focused on AI and quantum technologies. By investing in R&D, countries aim to stay at the forefront of innovation and ensure they have the necessary expertise to develop and deploy these technologies effectively.

Another important aspect of national strategies is building a skilled workforce. AI and quantum technologies require specialized knowledge and expertise, and countries are investing in education and training programs to develop a workforce capable of driving innovation in these fields. By prioritizing education in AI and quantum technologies, nations can ensure that they have a pool of talented individuals equipped to tackle the challenges and opportunities presented by these technologies.

Collaboration and partnerships are also key components of national strategies for advancing AI and quantum technologies. Countries are forming alliances with other nations, industry partners, and research institutions to share knowledge, resources, and best practices. By collaborating on research projects and sharing expertise, countries can accelerate the development of AI and quantum technologies and ensure they remain competitive in the global landscape.

Overall, national strategies for advancing AI and quantum technologies are crucial for countries looking to secure their position in the global race for technological superiority. By investing in research and development, building a skilled workforce, and fostering collaboration, nations can position themselves as leaders in these transformative fields. As AI and quantum technologies continue to evolve, it is essential for countries to stay ahead of the curve and harness the potential of these technologies to drive innovation, economic growth, and national security.

Chapter 3: The Implications for International Security

Cybersecurity Challenges in the Age of AI

In the fast-paced world of technological advancement, the integration of artificial intelligence (AI) has become increasingly prevalent across various industries. However, with this rapid adoption of AI comes a host of cybersecurity challenges that must be addressed in order to ensure the safety and security of sensitive data and systems. The intersection of AI and cybersecurity presents a complex landscape that requires careful navigation in order to protect against potential threats and vulnerabilities.

One of the major challenges in the age of AI is the potential for AI-powered cyberattacks to be more sophisticated and difficult to detect. As AI algorithms become more advanced, malicious actors are finding new ways to leverage this technology to launch targeted attacks that can evade traditional security measures. This poses a significant threat to organizations and governments alike, as the potential for large-scale data breaches and disruptions to critical infrastructure becomes increasingly likely.

Another key challenge is the ethical implications of AI in cybersecurity. As AI systems are trained on vast amounts of data, there is a risk of perpetuating biases and discrimination in decision-making processes. This raises important questions about the ethical use of AI in cybersecurity and the need for transparency and accountability in how these systems are developed and deployed. Additionally, the potential for AI to be used in offensive cyber operations raises concerns about the escalation of cyber conflicts and the implications for international security.

Furthermore, the interconnected nature of AI systems poses challenges in terms of managing and securing complex networks. As AI technologies become more integrated into critical infrastructure and industrial systems, the potential for cascading failures and widespread disruptions increases. This highlights the need for robust cybersecurity measures that can adapt to the evolving threat landscape and protect against potential vulnerabilities in interconnected AI systems.

In order to address these challenges, it is crucial for organizations and governments to prioritize cybersecurity in the development and deployment of AI technologies. This requires collaboration between stakeholders in the public and private sectors to develop comprehensive strategies for securing AI systems and mitigating potential risks. By staying ahead of emerging threats and investing in cybersecurity measures, we can ensure that AI technologies continue to drive innovation and progress while safeguarding against potential security risks in the age of AI.

Quantum Encryption and the Future of Secure Communication

Quantum encryption is poised to revolutionize the future of secure communication, offering unparalleled levels of protection against cyber threats and ensuring the confidentiality of sensitive information. As traditional encryption methods become increasingly vulnerable to sophisticated hacking techniques, quantum encryption harnesses the principles of quantum mechanics to create unbreakable codes that are virtually impossible to decipher. This groundbreaking technology holds the key to safeguarding the integrity of communications networks and securing critical data in an era of escalating cyber warfare.

The development of quantum encryption represents a significant milestone in the ongoing global race for technological superiority, with nations vying to harness the power of quantum technologies to gain a competitive edge in the digital age. As quantum computers continue to advance in complexity and capability, the need for robust encryption mechanisms has never been more urgent. Quantum encryption offers a solution to the growing cybersecurity threats facing governments, businesses, and individuals, providing a secure foundation for the exchange of sensitive information in an increasingly interconnected world.

The integration of quantum encryption into existing communication networks holds the potential to revolutionize the way we transmit and protect data, paving the way for a new era of secure and reliable communication. By leveraging the principles of quantum entanglement and superposition, quantum encryption enables the creation of secure communication channels that are immune to eavesdropping and interception. This level of security is essential for safeguarding national security interests, protecting critical infrastructure, and ensuring the privacy of individuals in a digital landscape fraught with threats.

In the context of international security, quantum encryption has the potential to reshape the dynamics of cyber warfare and espionage, offering a powerful tool for defending against malicious actors seeking to exploit vulnerabilities in communication systems. As nations increasingly rely on digital technologies to support their military operations and intelligence activities, the ability to secure sensitive communications and data transmissions is critical to maintaining a strategic advantage in the global arena. Quantum encryption represents a game-changing innovation that can help to protect against the growing sophistication of cyber threats and ensure the integrity of communication networks in an era of rapid technological advancement.

In conclusion, quantum encryption holds the key to unlocking a new paradigm of secure communication that is essential for navigating the complex challenges of the digital age. As the global race for technological superiority continues to intensify, nations must prioritize the development and deployment of quantum encryption technologies to safeguard their critical information assets and maintain a competitive edge in the evolving landscape of international security. By investing in quantum encryption research and infrastructure, countries can position themselves at the forefront of the quantum revolution and secure their communications networks against emerging cyber threats.

AI and Autonomous Weapons: The Ethical Dilemma

In recent years, the development of artificial intelligence (AI) and autonomous weapons has raised significant ethical concerns among experts and policymakers worldwide. The increasing capabilities of AI-driven technologies have made it possible for autonomous weapons to make decisions and take actions without direct human intervention. This raises questions about the ethical implications of delegating life-and-death decisions to machines, as well as concerns about the potential for misuse and unintended consequences.

One of the key ethical dilemmas surrounding AI and autonomous weapons is the issue of accountability. Unlike human soldiers, who can be held accountable for their actions on the battlefield, autonomous weapons do not possess moral agency or the ability to make ethical judgments. This raises questions about who should be held responsible for the actions of these weapons in the event of a mistake or violation of international law. Should it be the developers, operators, or the machines themselves?

Another ethical dilemma posed by AI and autonomous weapons is the potential for indiscriminate harm and violations of human rights. Without the ability to distinguish between combatants and civilians, autonomous weapons may inadvertently target innocent bystanders and violate the principles of proportionality and distinction in international humanitarian law. This raises concerns about the ethical implications of using such weapons in conflict situations and the potential for widespread civilian casualties.

The rapid advancement of AI and autonomous weapons technologies also raises questions about the impact of these developments on global security and stability. As more countries and non-state actors acquire and deploy these technologies, there is a risk of escalating arms races and conflicts, as well as the erosion of existing norms and regulations governing the use of force. This poses a significant challenge for policymakers and international organizations seeking to address the ethical dilemmas posed by AI and autonomous weapons while ensuring global security and stability.

In conclusion, the ethical dilemmas surrounding AI and autonomous weapons are complex and multifaceted, requiring careful consideration and thoughtful deliberation by policymakers, experts, and the public. As the global race for technological superiority in AI and quantum technologies intensifies, it is essential to address these ethical concerns and establish clear guidelines and regulations to govern the development and use of autonomous weapons. Failure to do so could have far-reaching implications for international security and the future of warfare.

Chapter 4: The Role of Governments and International Organizations

Government Funding for AI and Quantum Research

Government funding for AI and quantum research plays a crucial role in the global race for technological superiority. As countries around the world recognize the potential impact of artificial intelligence and quantum technologies on their economies and national security, they are increasing their investments in research and development in these fields. Government funding provides the resources needed to support cutting-edge research, attract top talent, and drive innovation in AI and quantum technologies.

In recent years, countries like the United States, China, and European nations have significantly increased their funding for AI and quantum research. The US government, for example, has launched initiatives such as the National Artificial Intelligence Research Resource Task Force and the National Quantum Initiative to support research in these areas. China has also made substantial investments in AI and quantum technologies through programs like the National Key R&D Program and the Quantum Exascale Computing Program. These investments are aimed at maintaining competitiveness in these critical technology fields.

Government funding for AI and quantum research not only drives technological advancements but also plays a key role in shaping international security dynamics. As countries develop capabilities in AI and quantum technologies, they gain strategic advantages that can impact military operations, cybersecurity, and intelligence gathering. By investing in research in these areas, governments are positioning themselves to address emerging security challenges and protect their national interests in an increasingly digital and interconnected world.

The global race for technological superiority in AI and quantum technologies is intensifying, with countries vying for leadership in these critical fields. Government funding is a key driver of this competition, providing the resources needed to support research, development, and commercialization of AI and quantum technologies. As countries continue to invest in these areas, the stakes are high, with implications for economic competitiveness, national security, and international relations.

In conclusion, government funding for AI and quantum research is a crucial factor in the global race for technological superiority. As countries increase their investments in these areas, they are positioning themselves to drive innovation, attract top talent, and address emerging security challenges. By supporting research and development in AI and quantum technologies, governments are shaping the future of technology and positioning themselves for success in the digital age.

International Cooperation in AI and Quantum Development

In today's rapidly advancing technological landscape, the race for superiority in artificial intelligence (AI) and quantum technologies is heating up. As countries around the world invest heavily in these cutting-edge fields, the need for international cooperation has never been more pressing. Collaboration between nations is essential to ensure that these powerful technologies are developed and used responsibly, for the benefit of all.

One area where international cooperation is particularly crucial is in the field of AI ethics. As AI systems become more advanced and autonomous, the potential for unintended consequences and ethical dilemmas grows. By working together to establish common standards and guidelines for the ethical development and use of AI, countries can help ensure that these powerful technologies are used in ways that are safe, fair, and transparent.

Another key aspect of international cooperation in AI and quantum development is in the sharing of research and resources. No single country has a monopoly on talent or expertise in these fields, and by working together, nations can pool their resources to accelerate progress and drive innovation. By fostering collaboration between researchers, industry leaders, and policymakers, countries can ensure that the benefits of AI and quantum technologies are shared equitably around the globe.

In addition to ethical considerations and research collaboration, international cooperation is also essential for addressing the security implications of AI and quantum technologies. As these technologies become increasingly integrated into critical infrastructure and defense systems, the potential for cyberattacks and other security threats grows. By working together to establish common cybersecurity protocols and information-sharing mechanisms, countries can help mitigate these risks and ensure that these technologies are used in ways that enhance global security, rather than undermine it.

In conclusion, the global race for technological superiority in AI and quantum technologies presents both immense opportunities and significant challenges. By fostering international cooperation in these fields, countries can ensure that these powerful technologies are developed and used responsibly, ethically, and securely. Only by working together can nations harness the full potential of AI and quantum technologies for the benefit of all.

The Need for Global Governance in the Age of AI and Quantum Technologies

In the rapidly evolving landscape of technology, the development of artificial intelligence (AI) and quantum technologies has become a focal point for nations around the world. As these technologies continue to advance at a rapid pace, the need for global governance has never been more crucial. The implications of AI and quantum technologies extend far beyond the realms of innovation and economic growth, touching on crucial issues of international security and ethics. In this subchapter, we will explore the pressing need for global cooperation and governance in the age of AI and quantum technologies.

First and foremost, the sheer power and potential of AI and quantum technologies have raised concerns about the implications for international security. The capabilities of these technologies, from autonomous weapons to quantum computing, have the potential to disrupt the global balance of power and create new security threats. Without proper governance mechanisms in place, there is a risk of these technologies being misused or weaponized, leading to increased tensions and conflicts between nations.

Furthermore, the ethical implications of AI and quantum technologies cannot be overlooked. As these technologies become more integrated into our daily lives, questions around privacy, accountability, and bias come to the forefront. Global governance frameworks are needed to ensure that these technologies are developed and deployed in a responsible and ethical manner, safeguarding the rights and well-being of individuals around the world.

In addition to security and ethics, the economic implications of AI and quantum technologies underscore the need for global governance. As nations race to develop and commercialize these technologies, there is a risk of creating new divides and inequalities on a global scale. Global cooperation and coordination are essential to ensure that the benefits of these technologies are shared equitably and that no country is left behind in the race for technological superiority.

Ultimately, the need for global governance in the age of AI and quantum technologies is a pressing issue that requires urgent attention and action. By working together to establish international norms, standards, and regulations, we can harness the potential of these technologies for the greater good of humanity. It is only through collaboration and cooperation that we can navigate the complexities of the global race for technological superiority and ensure a future that is safe, ethical, and prosperous for all.

Chapter 5: The Future of Technological Superiority

The Potential Impact of AI and Quantum Technologies on Global Power Dynamics

The potential impact of AI and quantum technologies on global power dynamics is a topic of increasing importance in today's rapidly evolving technological landscape. As countries around the world race to develop and harness the power of artificial intelligence and quantum computing, the implications for global power dynamics are profound and far-reaching. In this subchapter, we will explore how these emerging technologies are reshaping the balance of power on the world stage and what implications this may have for international security.

One of the key ways in which AI and quantum technologies are impacting global power dynamics is through their potential to revolutionize military capabilities. AI-powered autonomous weapons systems have the potential to transform the nature of warfare, giving countries with advanced AI capabilities a significant advantage on the battlefield. Quantum computing, with its ability to process vast amounts of data at unprecedented speeds, also has the potential to revolutionize military operations, giving countries with quantum capabilities a strategic edge in intelligence gathering and cyber warfare.

In addition to their impact on military capabilities, AI and quantum technologies are also reshaping the global economy and influencing the distribution of economic power. Countries that are at the forefront of AI and quantum research and development stand to gain a competitive edge in industries ranging from finance to healthcare to transportation. This technological advantage could translate into economic dominance on the world stage, with significant implications for global power dynamics.

Furthermore, the rise of AI and quantum technologies is also raising important questions about ethics, governance, and security. The development of AI-powered autonomous weapons systems raises concerns about the potential for unintended consequences and the need for ethical guidelines and regulations. Quantum computing, with its potential to break traditional encryption methods, also raises concerns about cybersecurity and the need for enhanced security measures to protect sensitive information and critical infrastructure.

In conclusion, the potential impact of AI and quantum technologies on global power dynamics is significant and multifaceted. As countries around the world race to develop and harness the power of these emerging technologies, the implications for international security, economic power, and ethical governance are profound. It is crucial for policymakers, researchers, and industry leaders to engage in thoughtful and informed discussions about how best to navigate this rapidly evolving technological landscape in order to ensure a more secure, prosperous, and ethical future for all.

The Race to Develop Practical Applications for AI and Quantum Computing

In the race to develop practical applications for artificial intelligence (AI) and quantum computing, countries around the world are investing heavily in research and development to gain an edge in these transformative technologies. AI, which refers to machines that can perform tasks that typically require human intelligence, has the potential to revolutionize industries ranging from healthcare to finance. Quantum computing, on the other hand, utilizes the principles of quantum mechanics to perform calculations at speeds far beyond what traditional computers are capable of.

The competition to harness the power of AI and quantum computing is fierce, with nations such as the United States, China, and Russia vying for technological supremacy. These countries are pouring resources into building the infrastructure and talent base needed to advance these technologies, recognizing the potential economic and strategic advantages they offer. From developing advanced algorithms for machine learning to building quantum computers capable of solving complex problems, the race to innovate in AI and quantum computing is driving a new era of technological competition.

The implications of this global race for technological superiority extend beyond economic prosperity to national security concerns. As AI and quantum technologies become increasingly integrated into critical infrastructure and defense systems, countries are grappling with how to protect themselves from potential cyber threats and ensure that their technological capabilities remain secure. The fear of falling behind in the AI and quantum arms race is leading to increased investment in cybersecurity and efforts to establish international norms and agreements to govern the use of these technologies.

The intersection of AI, quantum technologies, and international security is a complex and evolving landscape that presents both opportunities and challenges for policymakers and technologists alike. On one hand, the potential benefits of AI and quantum computing in areas such as precision medicine, climate modeling, and financial forecasting are immense. On the other hand, the rapid pace of technological advancement and the potential for misuse or unintended consequences raise important ethical and security considerations that must be addressed.

As countries continue to push the boundaries of what is possible with AI and quantum computing, the need for collaboration and cooperation on a global scale becomes increasingly urgent. By working together to develop standards and protocols for the responsible use of these technologies, nations can ensure that the benefits of AI and quantum computing are realized while minimizing the risks. The race to the future is on, and the stakes could not be higher.

Ensuring Ethical and Responsible Use of AI and Quantum Technologies

As the global race for technological superiority intensifies, it is essential to ensure the ethical and responsible use of AI and quantum technologies. These cutting-edge technologies have the potential to revolutionize industries, improve quality of life, and enhance national security. However, they also present unique ethical challenges that must be addressed to prevent misuse and ensure that their benefits are maximized for the greater good.

One of the key considerations in ensuring ethical and responsible use of AI and quantum technologies is transparency. It is essential for organizations and governments to be transparent about how these technologies are being used, the data that is being collected and analyzed, and the potential impacts on individuals and society as a whole. Transparency builds trust and accountability, which are essential for ensuring that AI and quantum technologies are used in a responsible manner.

Another important aspect of ensuring ethical use of AI and quantum technologies is privacy and data protection. As these technologies rely heavily on data, it is crucial to establish robust privacy policies and security measures to protect individuals' personal information. This includes ensuring that data is collected and used in a lawful and ethical manner, with clear consent from individuals and safeguards in place to prevent unauthorized access or misuse.

In addition to transparency and data protection, it is also important to consider the potential societal impacts of AI and quantum technologies. These technologies have the potential to disrupt industries, create new opportunities for economic growth, and improve efficiency and productivity. However, they also have the potential to exacerbate existing inequalities, disrupt labor markets, and raise ethical questions about the use of automation and artificial intelligence in decision-making processes.

Overall, ensuring the ethical and responsible use of AI and quantum technologies requires a coordinated effort from governments, organizations, and individuals. By establishing clear ethical guidelines, promoting transparency and accountability, protecting privacy and data, and considering the societal impacts of these technologies, we can harness their potential for positive change while minimizing the risks of misuse and harm. The global race for technological superiority must be guided by ethical principles and a commitment to responsible innovation to ensure a better future for all.

Top AI Companies in Leading AI Countries:

1. **United States:**
   - ○ **OpenAI:** Known for its advanced AI models such as GPT-4 and DALL-E, supported by a significant partnership with Microsoft.
   - ○ **IBM:** Famous for its Watson platform, IBM has a long history of innovation in AI across multiple industries.
   - ○ **Google:** A major player with its AI research lab DeepMind and applications in search, autonomous driving, and healthcare.
2. **China:**
   - ○ **Baidu:** Pioneering in AI-powered search engines and autonomous driving technologies.
   - ○ **Tencent:** Utilizing AI in social media, gaming, and financial services.
   - ○ **Huawei:** Investing heavily in AI for telecommunications and consumer electronics.
3. **Canada:**
   - ○ **Element AI:** Focused on making AI accessible for enterprise solutions.
   - ○ **Coveo:** Specializes in AI-driven search and recommendations for businesses.
   - ○ **Thales Canada:** Engaged in AI for defense and aerospace applications.
4. **United Kingdom:**
   - ○ **DeepMind (a subsidiary of Google):** Leading in AI research with applications in healthcare and energy efficiency.
   - ○ **Graphcore:** Known for its AI processors designed for machine learning tasks.
   - ○ **Babylon Health:** Utilizing AI for digital health and telemedicine.
5. **Germany:**
   - ○ **SAP:** Integrating AI into enterprise software solutions.

- o **Siemens:** Employing AI in industrial automation and smart infrastructure.
- o **Bosch:** Innovating in AI for automotive and home appliances.

6. **France:**
   - o **Dassault Systèmes:** Using AI for 3D design software and product lifecycle management.
   - o **Naval Group:** Implementing AI in defense technologies.
   - o **Capgemini:** Applying AI in consulting and technology services.

7. **South Korea:**
   - o **Samsung:** Leading in AI for consumer electronics and semiconductors.
   - o **LG Electronics:** Utilizing AI in home appliances and mobile devices.
   - o **Kakao:** Innovating in AI for social media and online services.

8. **Israel:**
   - o **Mobileye:** A leader in AI for autonomous driving and driver assistance systems.
   - o **NICE Systems:** Using AI for customer experience and financial crime prevention.
   - o **Checkpoint Software Technologies:** Implementing AI in cybersecurity solutions.

9. **Sweden:**
   - o **Spotify:** Leveraging AI for music recommendations and personalized experiences.
   - o **Ericsson:** Utilizing AI in telecommunications and 5G technology.
   - o **Volvo:** Innovating in AI for autonomous vehicles and safety systems.

10. **Singapore:**
    - o **Trax:** Employing AI for retail analytics and shelf monitoring.

- **SenseTime:** Leading in AI for facial recognition and computer vision.
- **Sea Group:** Using AI in e-commerce, digital entertainment, and financial services.

- **United States:**

  - **OpenAI:** Specializes in developing advanced AI models like GPT-4 for natural language processing and DALL-E for image generation. Its focus is on creating powerful and versatile AI tools for various applications, supported by a significant partnership with Microsoft (eWEEK).
  - **IBM:** Focuses on conversational AI and enterprise solutions with its Watson platform, which has applications in healthcare, customer service, and various other industries (Stash).
  - **Google (DeepMind):** Known for AI research and development in areas such as healthcare, energy efficiency, and reinforcement learning. DeepMind's notable projects include AlphaGo and advancements in protein folding (Analytics Insight).

- **China:**

  - **Baidu:** Pioneers in AI-powered search engines, natural language processing, and autonomous driving technologies. Their Apollo project is a significant initiative in self-driving cars (eWEEK).
  - **Tencent:** Utilizes AI across its platforms for social media, gaming, financial services, and healthcare, focusing on enhancing user experiences and operational efficiencies (Analytics Insight).
  - **Huawei:** Invests heavily in AI for telecommunications, cloud services, and consumer electronics, aiming to improve connectivity and smart device capabilities (Analytics Insight).

- **Canada:**

  - **Element AI:** Focuses on making AI accessible for enterprise applications, helping businesses implement AI solutions to optimize operations and decision-making processes (Analytics Insight).
  - **Coveo:** Specializes in AI-driven search and recommendation systems, enhancing user engagement and business intelligence for enterprises (Analytics Insight).

22

- **Thales Canada:** Engages in AI for defense and aerospace, focusing on improving safety, security, and operational efficiency through advanced AI technologies (Analytics Insight).

- **United Kingdom:**

  - **DeepMind (Google):** Focuses on groundbreaking AI research in healthcare, energy efficiency, and reinforcement learning. Known for projects like AlphaGo and protein folding advancements (Analytics Insight).
  - **Graphcore:** Develops AI processors designed for machine learning tasks, aiming to accelerate AI performance and efficiency in various applications (Analytics Insight).
  - **Babylon Health:** Utilizes AI for digital health and telemedicine, providing AI-powered diagnostics and patient care solutions (Analytics Insight).

- **Germany:**

  - **SAP:** Integrates AI into enterprise software solutions, helping businesses automate processes and gain insights through advanced analytics (Analytics Insight).
  - **Siemens:** Employs AI in industrial automation and smart infrastructure, enhancing operational efficiency and innovation in manufacturing and energy sectors (Analytics Insight).
  - **Bosch:** Innovates in AI for automotive technologies and home appliances, focusing on safety, efficiency, and user experience (Analytics Insight).

- **France:**

  - **Dassault Systèmes:** Uses AI for 3D design software and product lifecycle management, improving design processes and innovation in engineering and manufacturing (Analytics Insight).
  - **Naval Group:** Implements AI in defense technologies, enhancing capabilities in naval operations and security (Analytics Insight).

- **Capgemini:** Applies AI in consulting and technology services, helping clients leverage AI for digital transformation and operational efficiency (Analytics Insight).

- **South Korea:**

  - **Samsung:** Leads in AI for consumer electronics and semiconductors, focusing on enhancing device functionality and user experience through smart technologies (Analytics Insight).
  - **LG Electronics:** Utilizes AI in home appliances and mobile devices, improving convenience and efficiency for consumers (Analytics Insight).
  - **Kakao:** Innovates in AI for social media and online services, enhancing user interactions and content delivery (Analytics Insight).

- **Israel:**

  - **Mobileye:** Specializes in AI for autonomous driving and driver assistance systems, enhancing vehicle safety and efficiency through advanced AI technologies (eWEEK) (Analytics Insight).
  - **NICE Systems:** Uses AI for customer experience management and financial crime prevention, improving service quality and security (Analytics Insight).
  - **Checkpoint Software Technologies:** Implements AI in cybersecurity solutions, focusing on threat detection and prevention (Analytics Insight).

- **Sweden:**

  - **Spotify:** Leverages AI for music recommendations and personalized user experiences, enhancing content discovery and engagement (Analytics Insight).
  - **Ericsson:** Utilizes AI in telecommunications and 5G technology, improving network performance and connectivity (Analytics Insight).

- **Volvo:** Innovates in AI for autonomous vehicles and safety systems, focusing on enhancing driving experience and safety (Analytics Insight).

- **Singapore:**

  - **Trax:** Employs AI for retail analytics and shelf monitoring, helping retailers optimize inventory and improve sales (Analytics Insight).
  - **SenseTime:** Leads in AI for facial recognition and computer vision, focusing on security and surveillance applications (Analytics Insight).
  - **Sea Group:** Uses AI in e-commerce, digital entertainment, and financial services, driving innovation and growth in these sectors (Analytics Insight).

Top Companies in Quantum Technologies

United States

1. **IBM**:
   - Focus: IBM is a pioneer in quantum computing, offering cloud-based quantum computing access and developing powerful quantum processors. The company is working on a 433-qubit processor (Osprey) and aims to release a 1,121-qubit processor (Condor) (Home of Technology News).

2. **Google**:
   - Focus: Google Quantum AI focuses on advancing quantum computing for real-world applications. Their research aims to create scalable quantum computers capable of solving complex problems beyond classical capabilities (The Quantum Insider) (Home of Technology News).

3. **Microsoft**:
   - Focus: Microsoft's quantum efforts include the development of topological qubits and the Azure Quantum cloud platform, which provides access to various quantum resources and aims to make quantum computing accessible to businesses (The Quantum Insider) (Home of Technology News).

4. **Amazon (AWS Braket)**:
   - Focus: AWS Braket offers a managed quantum computing service, providing access to different quantum hardware through the cloud. Amazon also focuses on advancing quantum networking and error correction technologies (The Quantum Insider) (Home of Technology News).

5. **Rigetti Computing**:
   - Focus: Rigetti develops superconducting quantum processors and integrates them with classical computing systems. Their quantum cloud services make these resources accessible globally (CraizeTech).

China

1. **Alibaba Group**:
   - Focus: Alibaba is developing quantum computing technologies to enhance cloud computing capabilities and explore new applications in artificial intelligence and cryptography (The Quantum Insider).

Canada

1. **D-Wave Systems**:
   - Focus: D-Wave specializes in quantum annealing, a technique optimized for solving complex optimization problems. Their systems are used by organizations like NASA and Google for various applications (CraizeTech).
2. **Xanadu**:
   - Focus: Xanadu develops photonic quantum computers and offers access to these systems via the cloud. They focus on making quantum computing more accessible through open-source tools and integration with classical computing frameworks (CraizeTech).

United Kingdom

1. **Quantinuum**:
   - Focus: Formed by the merger of Cambridge Quantum Computing and Honeywell Quantum Solutions, Quantinuum develops trapped ion quantum computers with applications in quantum chemistry, machine learning, and artificial intelligence (CraizeTech).

Germany

1. **Atos Quantum**:
   - Focus: Atos Quantum develops the Quantum Learning Machine, a high-performance quantum simulator that helps researchers develop quantum algorithms applicable to various fields (CraizeTech).

Singapore

1. **Horizon Quantum Computing**:
   - Focus: Horizon Quantum Computing enables users to write programs in classical languages that can be executed on quantum computers, making quantum computing accessible to a broader audience (Built In).
2. **Atomionics**:
   - Focus: Atomionics develops quantum sensors for navigation and resource exploration, providing highly accurate measurements for underground and underwater applications (Built In).

www.ingramcontent.com/pod-product-compliance
Lightning Source LLC
Chambersburg PA
CBHW082125220526
45472CB00009B/2302

* 9 7 9 8 3 2 8 6 2 2 4 4 8 *